Bed And Breakfast Series: For Married Sistas Volume I

Lessons In Loving Your Boo to The Fullest

by

Antonio & Michelle Washington

COPYRIGHT © 2023 Antonio Washington & Michelle Washington

All rights reserved. No part of this book may be reproduced or transmitted in any form or by any means without written permission from the author.

Unless otherwise indicated, the Scriptures are taken from the King James Bible. The Authorized (King James) Version. Rights in the Authorized Version in the United Kingdom are vested in the Crown and reproduced by permission of the Crown's patentee, Cambridge University Press.

Cover (front) Art Created by: Gwen Cudek

V&G Publishing L.L.C.
P.O. Box 43702
Nottingham, MD 21236
www.vandgpublishing.com
vandgpublishing@gmail.com

Printed in the United States of America

First Printing Edition, 2023
ISBN 978-1-7361577-7-0

Bed & Breakfast Series, Volume 1

Table of Contents

Prologue 1

Chapter 1 My Love Awaits 3

Chapter 2 He Still Wants To Feast Upon You 9

Chapter 3 Don't Get It Twisted: Defraud is Not an Option 16

Chapter 4 Whisper Your Sweet Somethings to Him 25

Chapter 5 Trouble in Paradise 33

Chapter 6 Sistas Are You Married, But Livin Single? 38

Chapter 7 Sistas Don't Give Up So Easily: Let's Stay Together 46

Chapter 8 Become His Number One Profession 54

Chapter 9 The Seal of True Love and Its Enduring Flame 62

Epilogue 69

Prologue

"Within this Christian vision of marriage, here's what it means to fall in love. It is to look at another person, get a glimpse of what God is creating, and say, "I see whom God is making you, and it excites me! I want to be part of that. I want to partner with you and God in your journey to His throne. And when we get there, I will look at your magnificence and say, 'I always knew you could be like this. I got glimpses of it on earth, but now look at you!" (Keller)

Hello Sistas, I pray that you had a restful night's sleep and you have prepared yourself for the day by spending some quiet time and enjoying spiritual pillow talk with the Master. Today, we start one of our newest series entitled *Bed and Breakfast* for all of our married Sistas. Soon to be married and single, Sistas, waiting on your prince, take notes. We will be taking lessons from the one and only satisfying and sexy Shulammite Woman from none other than the *Song of Solomon*. It's about to get hot in here!!!! Aww, Sookie, Sookie. Hmmm.

Bed And Breakfast Series: For Married Sistas Volume I

Chapter One

My Love Awaits

The Song- best of <u>all</u> songs - Solomon's Song!

The Woman

"Kiss me-full on the mouth! Yes!

For your love is much better than wine, headier than your romantic oils.

The Syllables of your name murmur like a meadow brook.

No wonder everyone loves to say your name!

Take me away with you! Let's run off together.

An elopement with my King-Lover!

We'll celebrate, we'll sing, we'll make great music.

Yes! For your love is better than vintage wine."

(song of songs 1:2-4)

How hot is that, Sistas? I may need a moment. Contrary to what most would have believed to be true by customary standards of that day, the Shulammite woman was not timid and shy. And no Sistas, by any means, was her husband the initiator as our story begins. I love this woman because she has the hots for her man, and SHE is the initiator beyond a shadow of a doubt. You go, girl!!!!! I bet this Sista turned a few brothers' heads when they first read this amazing book. She had it going on—big shout out to the Shulammite woman. Let's give this Sista Girl her props.

She loved her Boo, and she wanted everyone to know it. She thoroughly enjoyed her intimate time with him and made no qualms about it. Look at this Sista; she starts right out proclaiming her love openly towards her man, lover, friend, and husband. Alright now!!!! Sistas, this is foreplay at its best. All day long, this Sista is pouring a deposit of yum yums into her man, which she is sure to get a return on. Oh, glory!!!

Modern-day "sexting" ain't got nothing on this Sista because she got her own unique telecommunication thing going on. She is layin' on the *Mac* for sho'. I love it!!!! She is in no way being prim or proper. She aims to let him know how she really feels about him.

Sistas, she and I must be related because even when I worked full time, I made it my business to send my husband little love notes throughout the day to get some things warmed up for the evening time, if you know what I mean. I would work on the brother all day long if I had to. I was a woman on a mission!!! And I still am. I love, love, love being intimate with my Boo, and you should too!!!

Sistas, it was not always this way. I am much more relaxed, secure, transparent, and liberated during those times of intimacy with my husband now. As a youth, I was sexually assaulted and had a lot of shame regarding intimacy. As a result, I was not always as comfortable in my skin as I am now. I owe the newfound freedom that I have obtained over the past seven years of our marriage to my husband because he pastored me throughout our marriage.

He knew about many things that I had gone through as a child, as far as physical abuse and the incident of sexual assault, and he ministered to me accordingly. He ministered to me without judging me or the people that imposed those things upon me. My husband took the time to listen, which allowed me to embrace my sexuality and no longer be ashamed during our times of lovemaking.

At the beginning of our marriage, I believed that my husband had to guess how I felt about him sexually because I was way too quiet, emotionally unavailable at times, and shy about it. I no longer hold back as far as letting him know how I feel about him before, during, or after our times of intimacy. And yes, our time together is so much more enjoyable. Shout Hallelujah with a Sista!!!

Sistas, I don't think that our husbands should ever have to guess whether or not we are sexually attracted to them, but so often, they do. So even though some of us feel they should already know this, I believe the only way they can really know is when we continuously communicate that to them. And yes, Sistas, there is that word again. **COMMUNICATE**.

I tend to flirt a lot with my husband, and we have a running joke between the two of us. I often tell him how oh so, very, very sexy he is, and he will jokingly say in a Jay-Jay-like from "Good Times" voice, "Well, you know, what can I say? That is what all the ladies tell me."And I, in turn, say to him in a joking but very secure, confident, soft, and sexy voice, "And they are so right because you got it goin' on, Baby."

Sistas, I know how to lay it on him. I often tell him. "You know babe, Justin Timberlake ain't got nothin' on you because you are bringin' sexy back." dunnin in nun (*my version of music playing in the background on the song, "I'm bringing sexy back" by Justin Timberlake*).

Okay, Sistas, by now, we should not be clueless at all about what they **NEED**. If they are indeed sexy to us, then guess what? They certainly need to **HEAR** it. They need to hear how so very sexy they are. Affairs can spring up when we are not telling them these things. I love this song by Robin Thicke, "Lost Without U," Listen to the lyrics, why don't ya...

"Tell me how you love me more. And how you think I'm sexy, Babe. That you don't want nobody else. You don't want this guy. You don't want that guy. You wanna touch yourself when you see me. Tell me how you love my body. And how I make you feel, Babe. You wanna roll with me. You want a home with me. You wanna stay warm and get out of the cold with me. I just love to hear you say it. It makes a man feel good, baby, Tell me you depend on me. I need to hear it."[1]

Okay, Sistas, if you don't know by now, this song was dedicated to his wife. How incredibly sexy is that? Hmmm. This brother here has a for-real handle on all that we need to know and practice tapping into when it comes to getting into the mindset of our mates. It is so very sexy. Sistas, try listening to the words more intently the next time you hear them. We can learn a lot from the words.

I asked my husband, the relationship expert, how he felt about this hot topic, and this is what he shared, "Whenever our wives let us know about how sexy we are or how they feel about us sexually, it affirms us. We, as husbands, need to know that we still got it. We need to know that we are still appealing to our wives. So often, wives assume that we already know how they feel, so they don't express it. Some women may not express this to their husbands unless they work out or are bodybuilders. Women will often tell other women how their husbands appeal to them but will neglect to let their husbands know this important tidbit of information." He continued to say, "Women need to not only focus on their husband's physical sexiness but on how inwardly sexy their husbands are. Inward sexiness consists of the way he talks to you, how he respects you, how he romances you, how he treats you, and how he shows his love towards you."

Okay, Sistas, is this true? Do you tell your hubby how sexy he is? Is he both inwardly and outwardly sexy to you? And how important is it for them to know how you really feel? These are your questions for the day.

Chapter Two

Your Beauty Is Way More Than Skin Deep:
He Still Wants to Feast Upon YOU!

Song of Solomon 1 vs. 5-6

"I am weathered but still elegant, oh, dear sisters in Jerusalem, Weather-darkened like Kedar desert tents, time-softened like Solomon's Temple hangings. Don't look down on me because I'm dark, darkened by the sun's harsh rays. My brothers ridiculed me and sent me to work in the fields. They made me care for the face of the earth, but I had no time to care for my own face."

Song of Solomon 2 vs. 4

"He took me home with him for a festive meal, but his eyes feasted on ME!"[2]

Hello, my Sensationally, Sensuous, Sassy, and Saintly Sistas; I pray that you are loving up on Jesus first and foremost, who is the

Lover of our souls. I also pray for you, married Sistas, that you have also taken time to shower your earthly Boo with some tender, loving care that only you can provide. I want us to take some time to look at the Shulammite woman again and glean from her display and example of the spiritual and sensual love she obviously had for her husband, lover, and friend. Enjoy!!!

As I told you before, I love this Sista. She is so transparent. Sistas, notice how she starts speaking confidently to her other Sistas about her appearance. She says, "I am weathered *but still elegant*, oh, dear sisters in Jerusalem, Weather-darkened like Kedar desert tents, time-softened like Solomon's Temple hangings. Don't look down on me because I'm dark, darkened by the sun's harsh rays. My brothers ridiculed me and sent me to work in the fields. They made me care for the face of the earth, but I had no time to care for my own face."

Look at this, Sista! How powerful is it to display such confidence among her haters, especially when she had to know that some of the other Sistas wanted her man exclusively for themselves, although they saw her standing right there? That sista was bold, for she says, "Sista's stop hatin' on me because I got a little bit of a tan. Stop sitting around at your little hate parties drinkin' your haterade talkin' about a sista cause she's got a tad bit more color than you. Hmmm. Sista's, I am still lookin' good for my man. And even though I had to be out in the fields when I was younger, my skin is still soft as a newborn baby's bottom. So, Sista's, don't let your jealousy blind you because I still got it goin' on. Haven't you heard that old but true sayin,' "The blacker the berry, the sweeter the ...."

Uh, Sistas, I hate to interrupt, but I just got one thing to say to this remarkable woman. *You go, girl!!!* This statement reminds me of how we often hide what we perceive to be our imperfections from our sweethearts. After having babies or just getting older, we often feel like we have lost some of our umph. But I submit to you that the older we get, the more refined we become, just like Chardonnay's most expensive and exclusive wines.

Sistas, with any good wine, it has to be fermented to tantalize the wine tester's taste buds. In other words, Sistas, we are at our absolute best as we age. Shout on, Sista, shout on!!! Sista, don't cover up the goodies from your man. Men are stimulated by sight. Trust me; this is not the time to play *peek-a-boo* when in maturity, you have become such a high commodity. We live in a society where the world is telling everyone else that it is okay to bear it all right before our men, and we need to let them know that we have it going on despite what's being boldly shown to them without their consent beyond closed doors. Our husbands love to see us display some bare necessities now and again. Oh, glory!!! Can I get a witness or two?

I pray that it is more now, more often, so that he won't be tempted by the one in the world who is not ashamed to show it at all. I know I am being pretty bold right now, but I ask you, when haven't I been bold enough to tell you the truth? Seriously, I minister to many women who are afraid to walk around in front of their mates unclothed. It causes some real issues because their husbands want to see them in all of their glory, despite the baby belly, stretch marks, and extra trimmin'.

Girlz, I mean to tell you, they seriously do not care about that stuff because they want to see YOU. They do not want to lust after someone else, but we sometimes give them no choice when we keep covering up! Now I am not condoning lust, but I am saying we need to fulfill their God-given stimulation no matter how we THINK we look. Okay? Somebody shout Hallelujah!!!!! Oh, I know that's right. They love having a confident woman who knows they have been refined throughout God's hands of time. I love this old song by Musiq, "Soul Child," which says,

"Lately, you've been questioning if I still see you the same way cause through these trying years, we gonna both physically change. Now, don't you know you'll always be the most beautiful woman I know, so let me reassure you, Darlin, that my feelings are truly unconditional. See, I'll love you when your hair turns gray, girl. I'll still want you if you gain a little weight. Yeah, the way I feel for you will always be the same, just as long as your love don't change. No, I was meant for you, and you were meant for me, yeah. And I'll make sure that I'll be

everything you need, yeah. Girl, the way we are is how it's gonna be just as long as your love don't change. Cause I'm not impressed, more or less, by those girls in the TV and magazines cause honestly, I believe that your beauty is way more than skin deep cause everything about you makes me feel I have the greatest gift in the world, and even when you get on my last nerve, I couldn't see myself being with another girl."

Okay, how powerful are these words? Most men are not concerned about the girlie girl in the magazines displaying all of their goodies as they are concerned about us not displaying our goodies before them. When we first got married and were without the baby add-ons, most of us liked how we looked. Well, we must maintain how we feel about ourselves throughout our marriage and learn to bear it all despite it. It's not so much that they will change the way they see us; it is more so that we change how we see ourselves, and in turn, our love for ourselves begins to change. And our lack of confidence can, in turn, change how we show our love toward them.

In conclusion, in Song of Solomon chapter II vs. 4 (msg), this Sista continues with her bold proclamations, still knowing that she is still HOT to her husband beyond a shadow of a doubt when she says, *"He took me home with him for a festive meal, but his eyes feasted on ME!"* She says, "I am still his passionately pleasing four-course meal along with the dessert and all of my fabulous trimmings, and it ain't a thing that anybody can do about it. Bon Appetit!!! Baby, Bon Appetit!!!" And Sistas, this is the exact same way WE need to feel about ourselves. "Sistas, your beauty is still way more than skin deep, don't change your love for him" Psalm 139:14 Praise Him!!!!!

Chapter Three

Uh, Don't Get It Twisted: Defraud Is Not an Option

Song of Solomon

"Ah, I hear my lover coming!

He is leaping over the mountains,

bounding over the hills.

Promise me, O women of Jerusalem,

by the gazelles and wild deer,

not to awaken love until the time is right"[3] *(vs. 8-9)*

Young Woman 2

"I am the spring crocus blooming on the Sharon Plain, My lover is

like a swift gazelle or a young stag.

Look, there he is behind the wall,

looking through the window,

peering into the room. My lover said to me,

"'Rise up, my darling!

Come away with me, my fair one!

Look, the winter is past, and the rains are over and gone.

The flowers are springing up, the season of singing birds (vs. 10-13)

"My dove is hiding behind the rocks, behind an outcrop on the cliff.

Let me see your face; let me hear your voice.

For your voice is pleasant, and your face is lovely. (vs. 14)

"Catch all the foxes, those little foxes,

before they ruin the vineyard of love,

for the grapevines are blossoming. (vs. 15)

"My lover is mine, and I am his.

He feeds among the lilies.

Before the dawn breezes blow and the night shadows flee,

return to me, my love, like a gazelle or a young stag on the rugged mountains." (vs. 16-17)

Song of Solomon 3:1-2

"One night, as I lay in bed, I yearned for my lover.

I yearned for him, but he did not come.

So I said to myself, "I will get up and roam the city,

Searching in all its streets and squares.

I will search for the one I love."

So I searched everywhere but did not find him."[4]

Hello, my Beautiful but Bold Married Sistas; I pray that you have been spending time with your first love, Jesus and that you are at peace and one with Him. I also pray that all is well with your earthly mate and lover. Let's continue with our series, which includes the Song of all Songs, none other than the Song of Solomon.

We are back with the most brazen woman that we know. This woman knows how to love her man. But like many of us today, she chooses not to shower him with her affection immediately. Hmmm. Like many of us, she has allowed something to get in the way of her intimate time with her lover. And that something drives a little bit of a wedge between them. Let's take a look and learn from her mistakes.

Sistas, notice her man, lover, friend, and husband are on a mission. He is in hot pursuit of his Boo. And she knows it. She even begins to give some really sound advice to her Sistas just before he begins to charm her, just like any real Sista that's got your back should do. She advises the Sistas not to rush into love too soon. Let love take its course. Wait on the right one for the right time. And this Brotha was obviously the right one for her. He was about to get hot and heavy. Woo!! Just like any Brotha, he is laying on the *Mac* for sho. He tells her to come away with him.

Okay, Sistas, it ain't nothing like a bit of afternoon delight. Can I get a witness?!!!! I feel like my help is coming on!!!! This Brotha is all into the change of seasons because Springtime has finally come. Woo hoo!!!! And we know how it is with Springtime. Love is in full bloom. He is ready to chill back and whisper some sweet nothings in her ear. But check this out. She hides from him.

(vs. 14) Say what now? Yeah, that's right. Sistas, I said she HIDES FROM HIM. Huh? Sistas, sometimes there are some things within that we are dealing with that will sometimes allow us to be ashamed or hide from our mates, especially if we feel as though we are not living up to the false expectations that are put in our minds by our greatest enemy, satan to bring division between our mates and us. But we must not let him. We must get a whole new attitude about ourselves by looking into the mirror of God's word to find out who He says we are and know that we have been forgiven and made new...... *"old things are passed away, and behold, all things are made new."[5]* His reflection never lies. And then there are also those times when we use our bodies as a weapon to get what we want. There are times when we are just being right out trifling with our husbands and holding back our goodies in an attempt to make them grovel or pay for the hurt that they may not even know was inflicted on a Sista.

Let me tell you something. Let me give you, Sistas, just a little bit of sound advice. I do not care what we are going through unless there is some abuse or adultery involved, which some Sistas would need to get to safety or find out which direction the Lord wants them to go regarding their marriage. But, in the meantime, if none of the above are going on, we just need to get it right with the Lord and our husbands because DEFRAUD (depriving or refusing your mate sexual intimacy) IS NEVER AN OPTION!!!!! Except fasting and praying; of which you both have to agree with or health issues. Are you feelin' me?

Go to Christian counseling if you have to. Talk to a respected Christian friend or mentor about the situation, but please, by all means, do not hold back the goodies. Trust me; what you are holding back, there is always another so-called Sista that will freely give it without reservation. WE cannot ever withhold sex and use it as a weapon to control our mates. That is witchcraft, and it is unbiblical. (See, I Samuel 15:23, I Corinthians 7:5, Hebrews 13:4, Proverbs 5:18, 19)

Even though this Sista was not responding correctly to her man for a minute, he still felt the need to be with her. So, this Brotha still proceeds to lay the *Mac* on. He tells her that he undeniably wants to hear her voice. So, he says, Speak up, baby, so I can come and love up on ya."

Now for some reason, this sista starts talking to her homegirls again right in the middle of her man, trying to get busy. Okay, Sistas, what is her problem? Cause I am going to tell you when Big daddy is calling me to some intimate time with him, I ain't got time to talk to the Sistas. I mean, I love y'all and erything, but I need to be with my man. And for real, y'all ain't gonna come between me and a little midnight rendezvous with my Boo. Ah, aw!!! I am here to tell you it ain't happening. Puleaze!!!

Now, let's be real for a moment. Many times, I have spoken with some Sistas that allow too many forms of modern technology to come in between them and their husband's intimate time. When he is ready, uh, trust me, it is not the time to be checking your texts, email, voice mail, etc.

Okay. Let's keep it real. Your girlfriend, the kids, and your momma can wait!!! Notice, at the beginning of her statement to the Sistas, in verse 15, *"Quick, catch all the foxes, those little foxes, before they ruin the vineyard of love, for the grapevines are blossoming."*[6] Okay, she is giving some real sound advice that she has yet to heed. Cause if she had taken her own advice, she would not have been hiding from the brother from the git. Okay?

Now Sistas, she quickly regains her seemingly sound mind when she begins to proclaim the unyielding love they have for one another. But guess what? It is too late for a Sista because Bro is nowhere to be found. Okay, Sistas, she just dissed him, so he had to be feeling rejected. And we know what rejection can do for a brother. That's right; it messes with his GOD-given ego. Sistas, don't hate on them. They are wired that way because Elohim, the great Creator, fashioned them that way.

Okay? Let's get back to the story. She then begins to look for him. My question to you is, is he ready to be found, or has someone else found him? We will pick this up again in the next chapter. But for now, Sistas, remember, as I have told you before, "Defraud is never an option." Make time to give that man your goodies and stop playin' with his emotions. I am only telling you this for his, your, and your children's good. Don't allow this nonsense to break up your God-given family.

Chapter Four

Whisper Your Sweet Somethings To Him:

The Importance of Words of Affirmation During Intimacy

*"A word spoken in due season, oh, how **GOOD** it IS!!!!!"*

Proverbs 15:23 (KJV)

Shhhhh!!! Pillow Talk Time..

The Shulamite (Song of Solomon 4:16)

"Awake, O north wind,

And come O south!

Blow upon my garden,

That its spices may flow out.

*Let my beloved come to **his** garden*

And eat its pleasant fruits."

The Beloved response (Song of Solomon 5:1)

"I have come to my garden, my sister, my spouse;

I have gathered my myrrh with my spice;

I have eaten my honeycomb with my honey;

I have drunk my wine with my milk."

Good morning my amazing, awesome Sistas; I pray that you are doing well by His grace and that nothing stands between your Savior and your soul. Sistas, as I lay upon the bed having a conversation with my Babe, I started dwelling once again on the importance of communication in marriage, especially in the marriage bed. I asked him this simple question, "Babe, how important is it for women to speak lovingly and openly share their feelings about their husbands during intimacy?" And he responded with the word that described what I was struggling to say as I was writing. The most amazing word that describes what most of us need resonated from his lips, the word "affirmation." Sistas, there is that word again.

The definition of an affirmation is *"emotional support or encouragement."*

Sistas, so many of us already feel so beat up from the world that we need a word spoken in due season. And it is equally essential for us to speak these words to our God-given mates, our husbands. So this morning, we will mainly focus on those awesome words of affirmation that need to be spoken during intimate time with our mates.

Sistas, our men need affirmation more than anything. Most people say that they need respect more than anything. I believe that this is so true based not only on what I had been taught and observed being lived out by my mentors but also in our marriage. I also firmly believe that we show them respect first and foremost by affirming them. Many of us do not take the time to affirm our husbands because our minds have become too busy with life. And to be quite honest with you, we often forget or don't even see the significance of it. Girlfriends, if you don't already know it, they really need this, especially during lovemaking. I love the dialogue between this husband and wife during their intimate time with one another.

Let's look at chapters 4 vs. 16 and 5:1, the Song of all Songs, this morning. Look at this Sista once again; she says all the right things to her Boo. This Sista is so sensual, and this Brotha knows it. She is laying on the sweet somethings. She lets him know how much she desires him and how he ultimately makes her feel. Okay, Sistas, let's all say it in synchronicity, "YOU GO, GIRL"!!!!! This Sista girl is free from all shame. She is not holding anything back. She is actually talking him through the process. Okay, Sista's, check this out *"Let my beloved come to his garden And eat its pleasant fruits."* Sistas, she is letting him know what she wants from him during their time of intimacy. Say what now????? To all of you shy, prim, and proper Sistas, take notes, please!!! Hmmm.

Sistas, I just got a stinkin' suspicion that her famous motto must be, "Ain't no shame in my game." And I love it!!!! And let me tell you why. We often don't express the things that we desire during intimacy. Some of us have secret fantasies of what we like to happen during intimacy within the bond of sacred intimacy. But, of course, I am so not talking about anything perverted. In other words, porn, chains, and whips are out of the question during Christian holy matrimony bonding time. Trust me, Sistas, if that is what you are looking for, you are on the wrong road. Okay!!!!!!!????? I forgive you, Boo.

Sistas, there are times when we don't really let them know what "floats our boat." Many of us have been involved in relationships where we may have had premarital sex, and there might have been this one person or more that may have done some things during sex that may have been desirable, and our spouse of legitimacy is not doing those things. Sistas, I am in no way validating premarital sex or those things that occurred with other men during premarital sex. But I think it is important for us to discuss the things that we desire during intimacy with our spouses.

Okay, you may ask yourself, "Why is Sista Michelle telling me this stuff so early in the morning? I have not had my coffee yet. Is she crazy?" No, Sistas, I am not. Okay. Let me tell you why I am telling you this. Take a look at II Corinthians 10:3-5. In other words, the enemy will play on a Sista's mind during intimacy about the shoulda,' coulda,' woulda's if she does not let her hubby know what she wants to be accomplished in the marriage bed. Let me break it down for ya. You may start fantasizing about an old lover and some things that occurred way back when if you don't get gutsy enough and speak up.

Ok, Sistas, that does not mean you just blurt it out and tell him everything he is not doing during that time. That simply means that you pray and ask God for the right time and opportunity to let him know what spins your world during times of intimacy. Okay. Now once he begins to do those things, of course, lay it on him; bring on the *Mac*, Girlfriend. Tell him how his special dose of the yum yums makes you feel. Sistas, you feelin' me?

And Sistas, if he is already doing those just right things, YES, he undoubtedly needs affirmation. So, step it up. Step up your game, Sista. It is good to make it known during intimacy what hits just that right spot in just that, oh, so right way. Now, how will they learn to keep doing a "good thing" if it is never expressed to them from the git? Okay???

This is why communication during lovemaking is so crucial. I cannot express to you the importance of affirmation any more than what I am doing right now. A simple "I love you," "I love it when you do that," or "I simply love the touch of your body or the way you touch me like that." I believe that whatever is in your spirit, the Holy Spirit tells you, or is on your mind to affirm your lover at that time, is appropriate. And yes, I said the Holy Spirit in that prior statement because, Sistas, He is there too. As a matter of fact, if you are having issues in the area of intimacy, you need to be praying with your spouse right before your time together.

Most of us know what to say, but we just don't say it. Girlfriend, I would even go so far as to say many times it may not be expressed to the other spouse what is desired during times of intimacy, so the other spouse is left emotionally and mentally unfulfilled because no words of affirmation were spoken, no pillow talk was whispered in his ear. Words of affirmation create an atmosphere of transparency. They elevate the chemistry between husband and wife. They make the communion during lovemaking that much more powerful because they amp up the intensity!!!! Woo girl, in the great words of Nelly, "It's getting **HOT** up in here."

And last but not least, as we see in Chapter **5**:1, when she affirms him, he, in turn, affirms her. You see, Sistas, real love reciprocates. Remember, *"A word spoken in due season, Oh, how **GOOD** (desirable; giving pleasant feeling) it IS!!!"* Proverbs 15:23

Oh, glory!!!! Oh, I know that's right!!!!!! Sistas, do not fail to whisper your sweet somethings to him. Make time for "Pillow Talk." There is importance in speaking words of affirmation during intimacy. Praise Him and him too!!!! Hallelujah!!!!

Chapter Five

Trouble In Paradise:

When Momma Ain't Happy, Ain't Nobody Happy

Read Song of Solomon 5:2-5:8

Hello, to all of my delightful Sistas; I pray that you are basking in the light of His presence this beautiful day and that you are filled to overflowing with Jesus' Joy. This morning, I woke up with the words "trouble in paradise" in my spirit. Sistas, if the truth be told, our bodies go through some crazy things as women. And our emotions can take us on a roller coaster ride that no husband wants to accompany us on. And guess what? When Momma ain't happy, ain't nobody happy!!!

Looking at Song of Solomon, starting with chapter 5 vs. 2, we see that there is definitely "trouble in paradise." However, it does not go into detail about precisely what happened, and that actually leaves room for the imagination. And it is a good thing it does. This couple, just like any other couple, is going through its ups and downs. Momma ain't happy, and neither is he. They are going through a misunderstanding, and emotions are heightened just when it looks as though a night of marital bliss is on the horizon.

Sistas, I am reminded of when I went through PMS issues and symptoms of perimenopause several years ago. Girl, it was pandemonium in paradise. I was meaner than mean and still can be at times. My hormones were all over the place. I would say and do things that I wouldn't usually say or do in my right state of mind. And Sistas, because my hormones were crazy, my sexual drive was and still is even crazier. This took my husband by surprise. And guess what? It took me for a loop too.

Sistas, I started wanting to be with my husband intimately a lot more often in the midst of being mean. Now you would think that would make the Brotha quite happy, but it actually threw him off a little. Picture this. His little meek, quiet, and somewhat reserved wife began to ask for quickies on a regular, and I almost liked to have worn that poor Brotha out. And in between me going on a rampage and going after his goodies every chance I got, I left him to believe that I was teetering on the brink of schizophrenia. Sistas, I still chase him around the house trying to get his goodies, so please stop blushing.

Now, in the beginning, he had a hard time comprehending that "Little Red Robin Hood"[7] had turned into the "Wicked Witch of the West"[8] with a side order of "She's Gotta Have It"[9] In the middle of the Brotha scratching his head and trying desperately to keep up, I realized that I had to tell him what my body was going through. I knew that I loved my husband deeply and did not want to get involved in an extramarital affair because I had unmet needs, so Sistas, I had to break it down to a Brotha. I was so determined not to be tempted to drag the mailman in the house on his midday run because I was so jacked up.

Sistas, I started by explaining to him what I felt like. I said, "Babe, I am seriously telling you. It is like an inferno up in here." Okay, Girlz, it felt like a two-alarm fire that had spread to 2/3 of the floors in a 15-story high building. Okay, Sistas, you get the picture. Right? I mean, I had to give that Brotha a for-real visual about the situation. And I did this more than once so that he would get it for sho'. Notice I did not nag; I simply sat him down and explained that I was a tad bit more sexual than usual and I needed more tending to so that Satan would not get a foothold in our marriage. I assured him it was not that I was interested in anyone else. But Satan was starting to have a field day with my mind, and I was not about to let him have his way, so the Brotha needed to step it up and help a Sista out in a for-real way.

Sistas, I got to tell you it was quite a transition because we must remember that as men get older, their libido may slow down. But after Big Daddy got the message, Sistas, I mean to tell you it was ON!!! Our intimate time began to be off the chain, and things got much better for us both. Momma was happy now, and so was

Mister. I was no longer as hot and bothered as I previously was, and my attitude miraculously changed. Girlz, once we were intimate, my hormones amazingly would regulate themselves. In other words, momma needed "sexual healing,"[10] and Doctor Babe was just the right man for the job. Sista Michelle, you preachin' **REAL GOOD**!!!! Amen, Sistas, Amen!!!!

Sistas, there are times when all married couples go through ups and downs, and this can be especially true during the change of life. But, Sistas, this is when we have to use our God-given wisdom, make sure the lines of communication are open, and continue to love up on our mates in the midst of our misunderstandings so that Satan will not get a foothold. Sistas, we all know when Momma ain't happy, ain't nobody happy. But he will see you through those times when there is "trouble in paradise" He is faithful in all things. Praise Him!!!!!

Chapter Six

Sistas, Are You Married But Livin' Single?

Song of Solomon 5:6

"I opened to my lover, but he was gone!

My heart sank.

I searched for him but could not find him anywhere.

I called to him, but there was no reply." (NLT)

Song of Solomon 5:8

"Make this promise, O women of Jerusalem—

If you find my lover, tell him I am weak with love."

Hello again, my amazing Sistas. Praise Him for another gorgeous day. I hope that you are doing wonderful and enjoying this day. I woke up with "livin' single"[11] in my spirit. Sistas, if the truth be told, many of us are married but "livin' single." We have committed before God to love "til death do us part," but we have not fully honored the words that were once spoken from our lips. So, Sistas, pray for your marriages and ask God today if any areas need to be worked on so that your marriage will fully represent Christ and the church together as one. He desires unity within our Christian marriages.

Sistas, many times in marriages, there is no accountability between mates. One spouse may leave and not tell the other spouse where they are going, as seen in the Song of Solomon 5:6. Look at this, Sistas; she asks all his homeboys and her homegirls where her honey was. Sistas, why is she doing that when she should know where her man is at all times?

Sistas, let me tell you something: No self-respecting Sista should be hunting her man down because she does not know where the heck he is. And Sistas, neither should he be looking all over town for you. There is this thing called checking in, and as married couples, we need to abide by it. That shows our mates that we respect them.

Sistas, look at this. The Brotha left out and had that Sistas mind reelin.' Okay, let brother try that with me. Girlz, back in the day before giving my life to Christ, his skull would have had a serious connection with my cast iron fryin' pan. His butt would have been sprawled out on that floor with a serious concussion because a **Sista don't play that**! First of all, before that Brotha left the house, he should have told her where he was going because communication is vital, especially when you are angry.

There have been many times when my husband and I have gotten into, uh, let's just say, heated *"moments of fellowship,"* and he would come to me and say, "I am going for a walk or a ride. I will be back." But, Sistas, he at least gives me the respect of letting me know where he is going and has sense enough to soothe any anxieties so that the enemy won't have a field day with my mind.

Early on in our marriage, I was the one that always wanted to reconcile when we were angry with each other. I was always the peacekeeper and often went to him to calm him down. I quickly learned that he needed time to process some things, and I needed to leave him alone so he could have peace of mind to think things through. As a matter of fact, I can remember one time when my husband and I got into a bit of a tiff at church, and he left out to cool down. An older, wiser woman saw me getting ready to go after him, and she said, "Let him go." Sistas, that simple gesture gave me the wisdom I needed to never go after him again but to wait until he cooled down and was ready to come back to me. Oh, I know that's right. Girlz, we do not have to keep going after them in desperation for fear that we may lose them.

Sistas, men, were made to be conquerors and, by all means, the pursuer. Being the aggressor all of the time can turn your man off. You need to give him time to build desire for YOU. So please chill out. He will lose all respect for you, and you will, in turn, lose respect for yourself when you constantly assume the role of pursuer rather than take on the role of pursued. In other words, a Sista should not be out pursuing her man; her man should instead be out pursuing her. When a woman pursues a man, she eventually will desire him more than he will desire her.

Younger Sistas, I know we live in a generation of liberated women, but you should not be texting and calling him 24/7. As a matter of fact, to keep that Brotha on his toes, there should be a little mystery in the relationship, and he should be calling you more. And yes, you should be able to look through his phone, emails, appointment book, etc., without him having any reservations, and he should be able to do the same with you. There are no secrets in marriage because when we keep things hidden and live separate lives, the enemy gets good and busy. So he should not still be talking to his old girlfriends, and neither should you be talking to your old boyfriends on a regular.

Sistas, let's go a little deeper......................even in the area of lovemaking, you should not always outdo him in getting the groove started. He should be coming after you for the yum yums too. In other words, he should be hot and heavy for ya, baby!!!! Some spouses lose the desire for their mates, which should not be so. Believe it or not, my friend recently spoke with a co-worker involved in a marriage where both spouses do not sleep in the same room. When we are not connected by sharing the marriage bed, it can certainly lead to an affair. And if the truth be told, deep down on the inside, some Sistas want to push their men out there. These Sistas want a biblical excuse to continue "livin' single" and eventually make it official so they can do their 'own thing' legally. Sistas that is just sheer witchcraft; manipulating a situation to get our way is straight from the pit. I don't even sleep well when Babe is not right next to me. I feel like there is something extremely important missing. Girlz, I need my Boo right there snuggled up beside me, and so should you.

Sistas, there are even those times when some Christian spouses may hang out with their friends as if they are single, go clubbin' (which we as Christians should not be doing anyway), and leave the other spouse at home. Sistas, say it with me, **"That is a**

big NO, NO." This is not how we do it when we have made a commitment before God.

Many of us have separate bank accounts, and we refuse to combine all household income. We hold on to that secret stash just in case things don't go well in our marriage, and then we can have something to fall back on. But, Sistas, this gives a place for the enemy to start something in a for-real way; if you don't believe in your heart of hearts that your marriage will stand the test of time and work by faith, neither will he and the enemy is banking on that.

Some of us are so determined to 'live single' that we keep our maiden name and never change it fully to our married name. Okay, Sistas, I must ask you this burning question, "Why do we get married if we are not willing to take on everything that belongs to him, including his name?" And then there are times when couples go on separate vacations and never share a vacation together. What's up with that? Girlz, we need time together with our Boo. There is nothin' like sitting back on the beach in the Caribbean Islands with your honey, sipping your Island drink and looking into each other's eyes and goin,' "Life is good, eh, Man?" and the other spouse is goin,' "Yeah, man, life is good."

Sistas, please remember that when we made that oath before God, it was not meant to be broken by 'livin' single.' Matthew 19:5 says, *"For this reason, a man will leave his father and mother and is joined with his wife, and the two are united into one."*[12] Girlz, the definition of "ONE" *is being a single entity of two or more components.* And that is the way it should be in our marriage. When he breathes, you breathe. When he starts a sentence, you finish it. Before he can get his thought out, you are already thinking it. That is what true oneness consists of. So, Sistas, make it your daily prayer and determination to never 'live single' in the bonds of holy matrimony.

Chapter Seven

Sistas, Don't Give Up So Easily: Let's Stay Together

Hello, my fantastic, fun-loving married Sistas in Christ; I pray that you are dining at the Master's table and allowing Him to shower you with His great love. He loves us so much. I encourage you to be steadfast and unmovable regarding your marriages today. My prayer is that you will trust Him through the ***process*** of becoming one flesh. Notice I said the ***process*** of becoming one flesh. Sistas, it takes a great deal of time, patience, and work to get through this process. And guess what, Sistas? We have to hang in there and continue to trust in the one who ordained this wonderful process of becoming one in marriage til' the end. He is able!!! Praise Him!!!

The Daughters of Jerusalem (Song of Solomon 6:1)

"Where has your beloved gone,

O fairest among women?

Where has your beloved turned aside,

That we may seek him with you?"

The Shulamite (Song of Solomon 6:3: key scripture)

"I am my beloved's

And my beloved is mine."

"Let's Stay Together"

"Let's, let's stay together

Lovin' you whether, whether

Times are good or bad, happy or sad

Whether times are good or bad, happy or sad."[13]

Sistas, there are those times when there has been a communication breakdown, tempers flare, and a period of separation occurs. Girlz, when we experience these seasons, our marriages may seem hopeless. We will often think within ourselves, *"Lord is this even worth it? Is our marriage repairable after all that we have been through?"*

Sistas, I submit to you that this is the point where we must begin to look beyond the here and now. We must look beyond our past pain and press toward the preordained future that He has in store for our marriages. Just remember, scripture says, *"As a man thinketh, so is he." Proverb 23:7*

Girlz, the destiny of our marriage can fall into the hands of an unhealthy thought life if we are not careful. In other words, if we ponder thoughts of death (divorce), we have already mentally eulogized that which God has proclaimed will live on until one or more partners' physical death has occurred. I have a question for you. If, He indeed *IS* "the resurrection and the life" and can speak life into any seemingly dead situation, then who are we to try to supersede the power and will of the Almighty One by speaking words of death into those things that He has supernaturally breathed life into?

Sistas, this is why He gave us the ministry of reconciliation so that we could be reconciled with one another regularly when we choose to walk in His great peace. Girlz, we also need to realize that when we speak negative things about our marriages and do not immediately make up our minds to change our speech, we give those negative things an assignment from hell to bring about some real collateral damage within our marriages. In this instance, we must begin speaking words of life, not death. *"Life and death are in the power of the tongue: and they that love it (the words that are spoken) shall eat (consume, take in) the fruit thereof."*

And if we look at Proverbs 18:20 (amp), *"a man's belly (ESSENCE, BEING) is filled by the fruit (outcome, result, product) of his mouth and with the increase of his lips shall he be filled (satisfied; made complete)."* That is a very powerful statement. We literally take on the persona of the words that we speak. We actually live by, or we live out, the words that we speak or the words that have been spoken to us or over us. So, for example, if any one of us has grown up in a home riddled with dysfunction and has experienced someone speaking negative words to us, we often live out the words that have been spoken to us until we allow the truth of God's word to heal and change us.

Sistas, I am trying to tell you that we need to get a whole new attitude about our marriages by not allowing our past disagreements and challenges to dictate whether or not we choose to live in wedded bliss with our mates. Or we can choose to live as though our marriages are "hell on earth" by allowing our speech to remain the same.

And to be honest with you, just as Jesus prayed for Peter when Peter was tempted and knew that Peter would eventually betray Him, we have to humble ourselves and pray for our mates. As a matter of fact, when Jesus first encountered Peter, his name was Simon which literally means *shifting sand*. Sistas, I know that some of us believe that our marriages are a bit too unstable and shift from one place to another. And we often feel as though our marriages are indeed existing in sinking sand. Still, I want to encourage you today that just as Peter's name was changed from Simon to Peter, which means rock or steadfast, so can our marriages be transformed from one of shaky ground to one that is steady, firm, and stands on the rock, which is Jesus.

Sistas, our husbands don't always get it right, and neither do we, so we need to get out of their faces when there is constant conflict and get into the face of Jesus with prayer because He is the only one that is powerful enough to change the situation anyway.

Look at the Shulamite woman. Even though she and her man just came through a major riff, she still wholeheartedly proclaims, *"I am my beloved's. And my beloved is mine."*[14] Ladies, she still proclaims him to be her lifetime Boo. Her love for him remains constant. Notice she refused to speak or consider words of death. She says to the Sistas (the Daughters of Jerusalem), "Girlfriends, we might be going through a little bit of a rough patch, but I still desire him and him only. He is my Boo "til the end." Sistas, the words, "I'm done with this," did not roll off of her tongue. She was in it to win it. I believe this Sista was much like the Sistas of old who would hang in there with their mates regardless of what came their way. This Sista chose to be an example to other women (The Daughters of Jerusalem) who looked up to her by remaining positive and hanging in there. Sometimes as younger Sistas, we give up too easily. After all, Girlz, why in the world would we put all that time and effort into our men and have someone else come along and reap the benefits of all that we have poured into them?

Girlfriends, getting to know someone else takes a lot more time and effort. I plan to be with Babe until the Lord calls either of us home. I am believing God for a double-width casket because I do not want to be left here without him. I always tell him, "Babe, if you go, I am going witcha, so make room." Trust me, Sistas, I am too old and tired to trade him in for a seemingly new and improved model. The grass is not greener with someone else. I would bet my last dollar that underneath that new man's turf (surface), he's got worms just like everyone else.

Let's face it; we have to begin to get a bird's eye view of our marriages. We must look at things through the eyes of faith by getting our focus off of what we physically see and instead focus on the manifestation of the spiritual as we walk this thing out by faith. So, Sistas, in the famous and profound words of Al Green, "Let's stay together"[15] in our marriages. Sistas, learn to love him whether times are good or bad, happy or sad. God has a great plan in store for your marriage if you just trust Him. Commitment to your mate and Him will keep you. Praise Him!!!!!

Chapter Eight

Become His Number One Profession:

Ain't Nothin' Better Than Makin' Up

Hello, married Sistas. Hallelujah! Praise the Lord! I woke up this morning with makin' up on my mind, and Babe is in trouble. Sistas, there are times when we go through moments of intensity in our marriages, and we need some real-time with our mates. Our husbands also need to know what makes us tick so that they will know how to diffuse some things. Let's take some time today and take some notes on how this Brotha became an avid student of his wife so that we will know how to pray for our husbands if they are not doing some of these things. Sistas, try not to get so frustrated; remember, prayer changes things.

Song of Solomon chapters 6 and 7 (key Chapter)

"How beautiful are your sandaled feet, O queenly maiden. Your rounded thighs are like jewels, the work of a skilled craftsman.

Your navel is perfectly formed like a goblet filled with mixed wine. Between your thighs lies a mound of wheat bordered with lilies. Your breasts are like two fawns, twin fawns of a gazelle. Your neck is as beautiful as an ivory tower. Your eyes are like the sparkling pools in Heshbon by the gate of Bath-rabbim. Your nose is as fine as the tower of Lebanon overlooking Damascus. Your head is as majestic as Mount Carmel, and the sheen of your hair radiates royalty. **The king is held captive by its tresses. Oh, how beautiful you are! How pleasing, my love, how full of delights!** *You are slender like a palm tree, and your breasts are like its clusters of fruit. I said, "I will climb the palm tree and take hold of its fruit. "May your breasts be like grape clusters, and the fragrance of your breath like apples. May your kisses be as exciting as the best wine, flowing gently over lips and teeth,"* (Song of Solomon 7: 1-9 NLT).

Sistas, look at this couple getting ready to get it on after some fierce moments of fellowship. This Brotha has been away from the Mrs. and realizes that he made a hasty decision and has to do everything possible to make this thing right. Once again, he is layin' on the *Mac* for sho.' He is saying all the right things to make a Sista want to melt in his arms and give up the goods for real. This had to be the best makeup session of all time.

Now Sistas, in order for this Brotha to lay the *Mac* on this heavy, he had to become an avid student of hers. In other words, all of her ways, everything about her, had to be on his mind day in and day out. He had to be mentally shadowing her minute by minute. He observed her just like a new employee would observe everything that he could from a seasoned employer.

Sistas, the definition of shadowing is a common form of job training that involves spending a lot of time with a seasoned expert while observing everything that he or she does that is related to the work that is expected to be accomplished as a part of the daily routine of the job. Girlz that Brotha knew that in order for him to score some for-real points with a Sista, he had to know what indeed made her tick.

Notice this Brotha literally started at this Sista's feet and went all the way to the crown of her lovely head. You go, boy!!! He really got into this Sista's entire existence of who and what God had created her to be and do. He described the intricate details of her entire being. All right now!!! I'm just sayin' the Brotha had it goin' on. That's what I'm talkin' about. He knew about everything that made her boat float. He was telling her all the specifics of all that he had observed. He described all that she meant to him without leaving out one minute detail. He said, *"Thou art beautiful in every way and in every aspect."* [16] In other words, Sistas, his theme song for his Mrs., was "I like it, like it, like it."

I said all of that to say this, men need to become avid students of their wives by listening to what they say, watching all that they do, and how they respond to certain things. Husbands need to know all of our likes and dislikes. They need to be admiring our hair, nails, and lipstick. They should compliment us regularly about the clothing we wear. But they should also be studying our eyes' facial expressions and know what we are really saying with our body language.

Sistas, they should be absolutely captivated by our beauty. Psalm 145:11(amp) says, *"The king is enthralled (spellbound, fascinated, captivated, enslaved) by your beauty; honor him, for he is your lord."* Okay, Sistas, in order for your husband to lay on the *Mac* like this and be mesmerized by you, you have to do something in return. In other words, honor him with your undeniable beauty and presence. He is your lord, and you were designed, formed, and fashioned by Elohim, our God, and Creator, to make him look so good. As a matter of fact, we are a reflection of his beauty which should be shining through us daily.

So, Girlz, take off the Molly clothes and wear something a little bit sexier and pleasing. Change your whole freakin' wardrobe if you have to. I mean, if you are wearing granny panties, a facial mask, and a bonnet every night, trust me, that does not raise his eyebrows except if it is a constant reminder of the previews from an upcoming horror movie. Please take Sista Michelle's advice and visit your local *Victoria's Secret* or lingerie store to find something that will spin his wheels and get some things churnin' a little bit, if you know what I mean. Do away with the flannel pajamas and mommy clothing. Lord child, that is why he keeps introducing you as his Momma. Spruce yourself up, for heaven's sake. Get your local Mary Kay representative to come over and teach you how to apply a little makeup. Sista, this is not "Night of the Living Dead,"[17] so fix your face, please. Get a spa treatment, try some new perfume, and a shorter skirt, not too far above the knees, though. I don't want to look like America's next top hoochie. Take an exclusive photo just for him and text it to him. Oh, come on now, don't play with me. There is nothin' wrong with sexting your husband as long as it is not vulgar. In other words, Sistas give him something to run home to not run away from. Please cut it out with the scare tactics; why don't ya!

    Sistas, you have to honor him with the way that you present yourself to him. Don't just wrap the gift any old kinda way. Present it with some dignity and some pazazz. Trust me, I ain't gonna be lookin' like my great old Aunt Gilda when it comes to lookin' good for Babe. But, I am giving that Brotha something to be proud of and feast his eyes upon. As a matter of fact, I could not tell you what a pair of flannel PJs look like cause' I don't wear them; AT ALL. You feelin' me? Sistas, when we are out and about walking around the Lord's great earthly kingdom, we should not only represent our great and mighty Lord and King, Jehovah, but we must represent our earthly awesome and wonderful kings with the way we carry ourselves. This includes our inner and outer appearance. Kingdom Divas, we must REPRESENT!!!!!!

Okay, Girlz, I am done for now, but I want you to ask yourself this question and pray about the answer before responding. Has your husband indeed become an avid student of yours, and are you HIS number one profession? Does he know all the right things to say when it comes to making up? If the answer is no to any of these questions, then you need to be praying for him with a trusted friend. To begin to do so, you must seek accountability, pray for accountability for him, talk to your Pastor or a Christian mentor about it, or you could possibly be looking like broom Hilda and need to get an *"Extreme Makeover."* Ain't nothing wrong with a little overhaul. Of course, Sistas, all of this is said in love. Smooches and praise Him.

Chapter Nine

The Seal of True Love and Its Enduring Flame

Hello, my magnificent married Sistas. Praise the Lord, for He is great and greatly to be praised. I pray that you are doing well today and have purposed in your heart to spend time in His presence, dining at the Master's table. There is nothing like spending time with Him. Well, I've had big fun teaching on our "Bed and Breakfast" series. It has been an *"off the chain"* experience, and I have thoroughly enjoyed myself. I pray that you have had some fun and gleaned from the experience as well. Today we are wrapping up this volume.

Sistas, I know that marriage can be difficult, and the journey can be rough at times but always remember that in the end, it will be worth the trip. You and your hubby are on your way to a profoundly awesome destiny. Jesus has provided the directions for you both to get there together if you just read the instruction manual that He has laid out before you both, written in His precious word, the Holy Bible. So don't lose faith now! He will be there to guide you through all things and get you to your final destination in Him. Trust me; He will not leave you in the state that you are in. HE IS SO AWESOMELY GOOD LIKE THAT!!! Praise His awesome and wonderful name!!!

Song of Solomon 8:6-7 (NLT)

"Place me as a seal over your heart or like a seal on your arm. For love is strong as death; jealousy as enduring as the grave. Love flashes like the fire, the brightest kind of flame. Many waters cannot quench love; neither can the floods drown it: if a man tried to buy love with everything he owned, his offer would be utterly despised."

Wow, Sistas, listen to those words in the scripture above. How wonderfully romantic to have your spouse whisper those words in your ear. Can you imagine you being placed as a seal over your Boo's heart or a seal on his arm as you walk through life arm and arm? A seal is defined as a device or substance that is used to join two things together so as to prevent them from coming apart or prevent anything from *"worn valve seals."*[18] Hmmm. "Worn valve seals?" What does that mean? According to research, worn valve seals are at the head of an engine. They open and close to let air in and exhaust out. The oil seal is a small cup that the stem of the valve goes through to keep oil from running down the stem and into the cylinder. It is shaped like an umbrella or an upside-down coffee cup. They wear out over time or get hard, and then the car will start to smoke. When it first starts, the oil runs down the stem when it is shut off and burns when the engine is first started. As a result, there is usually not enough oil for it to show while driving.

    Sistas, there are times when we are so weary from the enemy constantly attacking our marriages that we obtain worn valve syndrome. The seal of love given to us by the Father is meant to seal our relationships with our mates and bind us together so that we will remain as one no matter what comes our way. This valve to our hearts should only be opened to allow frustrations (exhaustion) to be released and allow relief from the fresh air of God's word.

When we don't do this, we become frustrated. Sistas, if we do not see the spiritual significance in this and how it applies to our marriages, just like that oil eventually begins to spill out everywhere, so will our emotions spill out everywhere. Sistas, we were designed to be emotional beings, and because of that, we will be all over the place. The fumes will be flying and spewing out everywhere. And guess what? There will be no one fanning the flame of resentment. The oil of gladness that once permeated our marriage when we first walked down the aisle will begin to run out because some things will begin to burn within. I can hear some of y'all sayin', right now, "Burn baby, burn." Talk about your 3-alarm fire. But, Sistas, you know this is not the attitude we need to have about our marriages. True love will keep us intact.

That is why the next part of that scripture makes it known that true love is stronger than death. Sistas, I don't care what anyone says; when we truly love someone with all of our heart and soul, death can't even separate us. To truly love someone like this, selfishness cannot remain a part of the equation. Selflessness is the characteristic that most strong marriages consist of. Girlz, it is no longer about you or him once you become one in holy matrimony. There is no such thing as 50-50 in marriage. Marriages require a hundred percent from us and a hundred percent of perseverance from our spouses. In this day and time, most often, selfishness prevails in marriages, and a marriage built on selfishness will not stand the test of time.

The next verse goes on to say, "Love flashes like the fire, the brightest kind of flame. Many waters cannot quench love; neither can the floods drown it." Sistas, true love is like an eternal flame. The fire never ever goes out. Girlz, true love burns bright with the light of the Savior shining through us. There is no such thing as falling out of love, not if you have both proclaimed yourselves to be born-again Christians. Remember, God is love, and anyone who undeniably loves another Christian, husbands and wives included, is walking in the light of Christ. Girlz, no one falls out of love; they just choose not to walk in the light, which ultimately affects their love walk even in marriage. Nothing can quench true love. The floods of adversity cannot overwhelm or drown (submerge, deaden, or cover) our marriages when we purpose to dwell together in true love.

It goes on to say, *"if a man tried to buy love with everything he owned, his offer would be utterly despised."*[19] So, women of God, please do not accept an offer to marry someone for all that he can financially provide for you. I mean to tell you, a sugar daddy is only good for a season because if that is the only reason you married him, it will not last. Sistas, bling is not everything. You looking like a diva and feeling like a store-bought made-to-order bride and gold digger is not worth it. Please, Sistas, I know you think living in a mansion on snob hill with the rest of the phonies is everything, but it is not. If you are going to marry, please marry for all of the right reasons, not for what you can get out of HIM, for, in the end, his offer to buy YOU and give you the world will be utterly despised. In the end, you will learn to hate each other, or he will still love you to pieces, maybe, and you will despise him.

Epilogue

Finally, Sistas, I want to encourage you to allow the enduring flame of love that Jesus showed you in dying on the cross for your sins to permeate your marriage. Just as He loves us with an everlasting love and draws us to Him daily, learn by His example and do the same for your Boo. Be patient with them. True Love, His love is an enduring flame and will never, ever go out, and neither should yours. Amen.

Antonio & Michelle Washington

Acknowledgments

We are very grateful for the village we have, which includes our parents, children, family members, siblings, church members, Pastor Tooten, and First Lady Charlene, that have done nothing short of stand beside us and cheer us on to use every spiritual gift we have to carry out the plan that God has for our lives. Thank you all for your faithfulness in being faithful armor-bearers and prayer warriors for our family. We could not have done anything without the Lord's great love and the caring and consistent hearts and souls of those around us. And a very special thanks to V&G Publishing for supporting our dream to become authors.

Endnotes

Prologue

1. Timothy Keller-The Meaning of Marriage: Facing the Complexities of Commitment with the Wisdom of God (2013)

Chapter 1. My Love Awaits

1. Eric Monte, Good Times (1970)
2. Justin Timberlake, Bringing Sexy Back (2006)
3. Thicke, Robin. Lost Without U Lyrics - Robin Thicke - lyrics007.com. https://www.lyrics007.com/Robin%20Thicke%20Lyrics/Lost%20Without%20U %20Lyrics.html

Chapter 2. He Still Wants to Feast Upon You

1. Musiq Soul Child. MUSIQ SOULCHILD – DON'T CHANGE LYRICS. https://www.songlyrics.com/musiq-soulchild/dont-change-lyrics/

Chapter 4. Whisper Your Sweet Somethings to Him

1. Nelly, It's Getting Hot in Herre (2002)
2. The definition of affirmation is "emotional support, encouragement" (Oxford Language)

Chapter 5. Trouble in Paradise

1. Charles Perrault, Little Red Riding Hood, (17th century)
2. L Frank Baum, The Wonderful Wizard of Oz. (1900)
3. Spike Lee, She's Gotta Have IT (1986)
4. Marvin Gaye, Sexual Healing (1982)

Chapter 7. Sistas, Don't Give Up So Easily: Let's Stay Together

1. Al Green, Let's stay together (1972)

Chapter 8. Become His Number-One Profession

1. George A. Romero, Night of the Living Dead (1968)

Chapter 9. The Seal of True Love and Its Enduring Flame

1. Oxford Language, s.v. "seal"

www.ingramcontent.com/pod-product-compliance
Lightning Source LLC
LaVergne TN
LVHW041550070426
835507LV00011B/1018